Judicial Beatitudes

of the
Ancient and Noble
Art of Judging

Judicial Beatitudes
of the
Ancient and Noble
Art of Judging

By

Hollis McGehee
Senior Status Judge

GRACE PUBLISHING, BROOKLYN MS

ISBN: 978-0-9981884-2-3

Contents

A good simple read for the 'judge' in every person.

Judicial Beatitudes are not just good attitudes for judges but for all of us.

Judicial Beatitudes was written to help me be a better judge but it presents on a much broader stage: How to live life in relation to others just as we want them to live in relation to us.

Judicial Beatitudes is a well defined word picture of the type judge I aspired to be. Moreover, Judicial Beatitudes is a description of how we should all approach our work in whatever field of work we find ourselves. Seeing our work, on the bench or any other field of endeavor, as an opportunity to serve is foundational to getting it right in the judicial branch of government and whatever life path you are on. The "beatitudes" presented here are good Judicial Beatitudes but also foundational principles for all people in all fields of employment and life in general. Being on time, showing respect to all people, being kind, being fair and courteous and all of the other principles urged here ought to be prayers for how we would want to live each day of our lives. Simply put, Judicial Beatitudes reflect the Golden Rule, "do unto others as you would have them do unto you." because every principle contained here is simply how we want to be treated by our judge, our spouse, our parents, our children, our doctor, our teacher, our plumber and our friends. These beatitudes are good for all of us in every area of our lives

Author's Note

THROUGH ALL OF TIME AND history the deep troubles of humanity have been brought to men and women for judicial solutions. Across these thousands of years, men and women of the judiciary have earnestly sought answers to the disputes of their fellowman. Judges have genuinely endeavored to be peacemakers, to seek and provide solutions to the deeply disturbing challenges of those who come to them. The efforts of appointed "judges" to help others resolve life's most difficult challenges has been the stage upon which the art of judicial resolution has developed. The artistic process has not and will never reach perfection because the very ones charged to carry on the process are likewise saddled with the imperfections of all of their fellow human beings. The ongoing pursuit of improving the artistic development in the field of the judiciary is the purpose and goal of this writing.

In spite of our disability of imperfection, judges might yet continue to develop and improve the art of judicial resolution by employing established life principles. This simple work, *Judicial Beatitudes*, seeks to bring together basic life principles for the benefit of all who bring their troubles to the judiciary for resolution. There is no doubt that many arrive before the bench against their will, but the reality is that the art of judging is still the best option for assisting and serving others. The improvement of this fine art is a goal well worth the effort. The purpose of this writing is lofty but necessary—to improve our service to our fellows. Judging, properly approached and carried out, is a "laying down" of one's life in service to others.

Preface

The next day Moses took his seat to serve as judge for the people, and they stood around him from morning till evening. When his father-in-law saw all that Moses was doing for the people, he said, "What is this you are doing for the people? Why do you alone sit as judge, while all these people stand around you from morning till evening?"

Moses answered him, "Because the people come to me to seek God's will. Whenever they have a dispute, it is brought to me, and I decide between the parties and inform them of God's decrees and instructions."

Moses' father-in-law replied, "What you are doing is not good. You and these people who come to you will only wear yourselves out. The work is too heavy for you; you cannot handle it alone. Listen now to me and I will give you some advice, and may God be with you. You must be the people's representative before God and bring their disputes to him. Teach them his decrees and instructions, and show them the way they are to live and how they are to behave.

*But select capable men from all the people—
men who fear God, trustworthy men who hate
dishonest gain—and appoint them as officials
over thousands, hundreds, fifties and tens. Have
them serve as judges for the people at all times,
but have them bring every difficult case to you;
the simple cases they can decide themselves.
That will make your load lighter, because they
will share it with you. If you do this and God so
commands, you will be able to stand the strain,
and all these people will go home satisfied."*

(Exodus 18:13-23)

The art of judicial resolution is an ancient practice.
Moses was not trained as a judge; he learned the art of
judging by serving daily. Jethro, Moses' sheepherding
father-in-law, upon observing Moses' service to the
people, gained great and valuable insight into the art
of judging. Jethro observed to Moses that there were
more efficient and effective ways to address the problems of the people. The advice Jethro gave Moses
accelerated and improved the process of judicial resolution. The goal of this writing is to encourage judges
and all interested in the art of judicial resolution to seek
a higher and better level of judicial performance.

The work of the judiciary is not carried out on clay or
paper; it is a mosaic performed upon the most valuable
tapestry, the very lives of fellow human beings. Thus we
are compelled to seek to learn and to strive to improve
this most vital art form. My sincere hope is that this writing picks up where Jethro left off and carries us to a higher level of artistry in this ancient calling of judging. I have
learned much from the writing and now I want to apply
what I have learned. I hope the same for all who answer
the call to the bench, to serve all who come for help with
our highest and best, and even higher and better yet.

Introduction

People Want and Deserve Good Judges

JUDGES ARE SERVANTS OF THE people. The people need and deserve a judge who brings his or her very best to the noble calling of the work of the judiciary. Judging is so demanding, so multifaceted, only those who are fully committed can perform the art of judging at a level worthy of the calling. The only proper motive to serve in the judiciary is just that simple: the desire to serve others. A willingness to give your best is the only good and true foundation for a judicial career.

The challenges and joy of serving in the judiciary have compelled this account of judicial beatitudes. It is the clear recognition of my own shortcomings and misgivings that gave birth to this work. I freely and fully acknowledge that much if not all of this writing is gleaned, at least in part, from my own shortcomings as a judge. Many who have worked with me will likely proclaim my inadequacy to write on this subject; I confess the righteousness of their complaint. However, it is in the trying and the failing, the successes born from failure, that one begins to learn how to reach higher and further. I am writing of goals rather than accomplishments. I am writing because I want to better learn this ancient art of judging. I want to better learn the skills of judging. Finding myself closer to the end than the beginning, my hope and desire are to encourage others to seek a higher level of service.

I believe I was called to write this account, these principles, the "beatitudes" of judging. The compulsion to write this came upon me sudden and strong, and its first draft flowed almost immediately. The process since the initial thought has been careful and thoughtful, but the sense of the need has grown ever stronger. The people of the judiciary, the judges and all those who work alongside them, are by and large a caring group of people who really want to do it well—in our hearts we want to be the kind of judge described in this work.

Here is a fact you learn only after you bow to serve others as a part of the judiciary: Just as he who first ate an oyster traveled into the unknown, so we as judges find ourselves in territory we have never been and frankly are not prepared for. Yes, there are schools for judges, most of them quite good; however, the art of effective judging is not learned in a book or a class but daily upon a bench when facing personal tragedy upon personal tragedy suffered by or upon those who come before you. When you take your place on the bench, you quickly learn that you are, more often than not, meeting your fellow man and woman at a place of deep hurt, darkness, and need. There is no formula to follow; there is no textbook to rely on for how to respond to these great needs. You are called upon to "fix" the un-fixable.

The heartfelt desire here is to seek to lay out some basic tools, which are absolutely essential to help judges carry on the art of the judiciary upon a canvas of service to others. We have and will daily encounter people at their best and worse. The potential for error and harm is ever present and at a high level. Troubling yet inevitable is the reality that we will not always be the judges the people so greatly need. A strong desire and hope to meet the needs of others should be our driving force in seeking to carry out our work at the highest level of humble service. The only proving ground for judges is in the courtroom where people facing life-sized problems are looking for a patient, kind, and honest judge to listen and reach a decision that is helpful and fair. We want to be judges who respond consistently well to the needs of others.

In order to be our very best, we need judicial beatitudes, principles to help guide us in our service. We need these principles to guide judges as they learn and carry out the art of judging. These judicial beatitudes are core values and principles for all who pursue this noble and ancient art. I would respectfully suggest these beatitudes, these principles, paint a portrait of the judge we should all aspire to be. The people in every nation deserve judges who embody these high principles. I can say with assurance, the application of these principles to our daily work will move us toward an improved judiciary serving the people who come before us in times of great trials and tribulations.

Finally, and maybe most importantly, the art of judging allows our paths to intersect with the paths of others. The sum total of our life's work is comprised of a finite number of these encounters. We must not yield to the urgency of the moment and thus miss the opportunity of investing our highest and best into the lives of those whose paths we cross. When we give our best, when we carry out our work with the right judicial attitudes and actions, we are all greatly enriched through the experience of the precious moments represented by each and every one of our encounters with the people in the courts. There will come a day when we no longer have the privilege to serve; it is then we will reflect on the paths we chose over our careers. Did we choose to serve the path of patience, kindness, and fairness, or did we give in to the more well-worn and hurried paths of life. Setting aside whatever choices we have made in the past, may we firmly resolve in this quiet moment, going forward: "We are here to serve by investing our very best in our work and the lives of others."

Beatitudes of Judging

A judge should:

BE A SERVANT

A judge serves the people, so we must approach our work as servants. The business of the court is not "our business"; it is the business of those we are elected or appointed to serve, people who come to us in times of great trial and tribulation in their lives. Judges are called to serve.

BE PREPARED

A judge who prepares well serves exceedingly well. Preparation is an integral part of the art of judging, a basic requirement and necessity of judging well. The people we serve both need and deserve judges who are well prepared.

BE DILIGENT

Diligence by the judiciary is a necessity. A judge must be diligent in all he or she does. The lives of the people affected by your work deserve the highest level of diligence.

BE WISE

Judges need to be wise in thought, word, and deed. Judges are required to read and know the law, but wisdom goes beyond just knowing the law. The wisdom necessary for the art of judging is acquired over a lifetime of learning by studying but also by experiencing and observing life. There have been many who have gone before us whose writing and their very lives demonstrate wisdom. We do well to study them all. Wisdom is a foundational key to a judge's service. Judges must use their hearts, minds, and mouths judiciously and wisely.

BE ON TIME

Judges who respect everyone's time and are themselves on time demonstrate a servant's heart and respect for all. Judges must be on time.

BE HUMBLE

The noble art of judging is built upon the principle of humble service. The system does not exist to serve the judge; the most basic foundational principle of the judicial system is judges who are humbly serving all the people who come seeking justice.

BE PROMPT

Justice delayed is truly justice denied. Judges must not put off until tomorrow what can be done today. The business before us is not ours to delay. Justice cries out for timely delivery. Judges must seriously endeavor to be prompt in their work!

BE GENTLE

Judges can and must treat other people the way we want to be treated. We must treat all who come before us and all who work with us the very way we want and expect to be treated. Judges can and must treat other people with gentleness.

BE KIND

Kindness is appropriate in every facet of life; the art of judging is no exception. Judges can and must be kind in even the most difficult of circumstances. Judges can and must be kind to all the people all the time.

BE PATIENT

Patience is a core principle for judging. Judges have to work patiently at their profession. When judges lose patience, their effort ceases to be an art; it ceases to be justice. The present moment is the most important moment in life—no one and nothing is more important than the present and the people who are before you. Judges must be patient to all in all they do.

BE HONEST

Judges have to be honest! Honesty should permeate every aspect of the art of judging. Judges must vigilantly guard against anything that gives even an appearance of undermining complete honesty in the judiciary.

BE FAIR

Fairness is the most foundational of all judicial principles. A judge must be fair to all, at all times and in all things. Judges must carefully listen, thoughtfully consider, and then fairly decide every matter.

A judge is a servant who is well prepared, diligent, and wise in all that is done; a judge must be on time, humble, and prompt in everything; a judge must be gentle, kind, and patient with and to all as well as absolutely honest and fair.

This is a portrait of the judge all should strive for. It is this portrait and the clear understanding that I do not fit in that frame that motivated this writing. I am not there yet, but forgetting the failures that lie behind, I must press on to pursue this goal of being the judge I am called to be, making this my daily goal in every matter, with every person. May it be so with all who are called to the bench, to this art of judging.

Chapter 1

A Judge Should Be a Servant

A judge serves the people, so we must approach our work as servants. The business of the court is not "our business"; it is the business of those we are elected or appointed to serve, people who come to us in times of great trial and tribulation in their lives. Judges are called to serve.

A SERVANT? FEW WILL SAY THEY have their heart set on serving others. In today's world, who sets as their life's goal: "I want to be a servant"? Admittedly it doesn't sound very attractive on its face, but we must examine the concept and reality of a servant more closely.

No matter one's religious preference or lack thereof, the world recognizes Jesus Christ as a great example of one who gave himself to serve others. Jesus said, "Whoever wants to become great among you must be your servant. . . . [Then referring to himself, he went on to say,] The Son of Man came not to be served, but to serve, and to give his life as a ransom for many"

(Matthew 20:26, 28). If Jesus, the most well-known central figure ever, said he came to serve, then judges can and, I would argue, must do the same—give our lives in service to others.

What does it mean to be a servant? Simply put, a servant is "a person working in the service of another." Just how does being a servant fit in with "All rise for the Honorable Judge. . . . Your Honor, may I be heard? Your Honor, may I approach the bench?" The "honor" lies in service well performed. When a judge sees the work of judging as a means of serving, then he or she truly serves with honor.

True honor lies not in serving oneself but in serving others. The goal is not to receive honor but to give honor to our fellow men and women by serving them with honor. The principles put forth here—serving others with honor, sensitivity, and respect to and for all—lay a foundation for serving with honor. Judges are called to serve, serving others in times of great need.

Serving with your whole heart is the key to serving well. The serving of others above self is answering the true call to the bench. The heart of a servant is not anyone's natural condition, but setting our minds on living this out can develop a heart of service: serving selflessly and sacrificially. When we as judges live out the attitudes suggested and encouraged here, we will find our hearts becoming servant oriented.

Judges must approach their daily work with this simple goal: "How can I best serve the people who have business before the court today?" The compelling motive has to be the needs of others. The judge's daily question to himself or herself is simply this: "How can I conduct the business of the court today so as to best accommodate the needs of those I was elected or appointed to serve?"

Every individual judge has different circumstances as to where, when, with whom, and how he or she does the work of that particular judicial position. There is no "one size fits all" plan that will work for how to be a judge who serves well. We need to one and all carefully and critically look at how our schedules, our hours, our court calendars, and the method of arranging the flow of the people's business to and through the courts will best meet the needs of those we serve. Then we must, with a servant's heart, make adjustments that the needs of others require. The practice of serving others and making adjustments to make our service better, more effective, and thus honor those we serve gives us our best opportunity to be the judge the people need and the one they deserve.

When a judge's tenure is over, his or her work is characterized by this question: "How long did you serve on the bench?" When we reflect on that question, our hearts will find greatest peace when those reflections reveal we sought to serve others. The only way to serve on the bench is to approach every aspect of our work with a servant's heart.

Chapter 2

A Judge Should Be Prepared

A judge who prepares well serves exceedingly well. Preparation is an integral part of the art of judging, a basic requirement and necessity of judging well. The people we serve both need and deserve judges who are well prepared.

"Counselor, would you please state the nature of your client's case?"

IMAGINE THIS IS YOUR DAY in court; you have looked forward to this day for a long time. You are finally facing the judge you are relying on to hear and decide your case. You have asked many questions about this judge and have come to believe this judge will take your case very seriously. Nothing in your life is more important than this very moment, and your judge begins the day by asking your lawyer what the case is about. You think, "What is my case about? What does he mean? I have spent more than a year waiting to get before this judge, I have paid my lawyer more than I could afford, and the judge asks what is the case about?" Imagine the disappointment and maybe even terror this strikes into the heart of the litigant who now is forced to the realization the very person who they were counting on doesn't even know what the case is about!

Preparation is not just for lawyers—it's for judges too! A judge should be well acquainted with the matters coming before the court. Judges need to have thoroughly familiarized themselves with each case to the full extent the canons of judicial ethics permit. Judges must make every effort to read, study, and carefully review the matter as if it were their own case. Judges cannot just rely on the lawyers to brief them on the case as they take the bench. Judges have a duty to the litigants, to the lawyers, and to the judiciary to be prepared to the full extent reasonably possible.

The "matter at hand" is not a matter at all; it's not "my case." The matter before us represents very real and frequently difficult life circumstances of real people just like us. People who come into the courts expect and deserve a judge who is fully prepared to hear and rule on their legal business, which is vitally crucial to them and their families.

The demands of the job are great. Judges can and surely will argue that it is just not reasonable to expect them to be prepared for every case—"My docket is so large." With few exceptions, most judges are overloaded, the docket facing them is daunting, and their other administrative responsibilities are immense. In spite of those real and immediate concerns, the lives of the people coming before us and the serious nature of their legal issues demand we are organized and all set to hear and dispose of their case.

Justice should not be circumstantial. People should

not be limited to receiving a judge's best just on the slow days when time permits for more preparation. Preparation by the judge is a vital prerequisite to justice for all appearing before the court. This is how vital this issue is: If the docket does not afford us sufficient time to be prepared, then we change the docket, not the standard of justice. The well-being, life, and liberty of others is at stake; judges have an absolute duty to be prepared. Arriving at court in time for the administrator to hand the judge his or her docket while walking briskly down the hall, robes billowing, chatting with colleagues on the way into the courtroom is not acceptable preparation for a properly prepared judge seeking to serve.

Judges are ultimately responsible for their work. The judge is required, regardless of any other factor, to be prepared to mete out justice in an effective and prepared manner. When judges fail to fully and effectively prepare, it reflects poorly on the very system we exist to serve. When we are not prepared, it sends a message to all that their case is just "one more matter on the court's docket." The reality is this is not a case but a very difficult landmark in the life of all involved.

My father, Mayes McGehee, was the best-prepared lawyer I ever observed in court. He left no stone unturned. The judges he appeared before knew this, and he made them better judges. We as judges need to—in fact, we must—encourage our lawyers to be fully prepared, and the best way for that to happen is for them to know we are fully prepared. There is a trend to approach the law as a "business" transaction. We must do our part to return the practice of law and the judging of those matters to the noble art form it evolved from. The very best way to encourage the lawyers in their preparation is for us to be fully prepared.

When the lawyers know the judge is ready, they too will by and large be fully prepared. They are encouraged to be prepared because they know the judge is on top of the facts and the law of the case. Well-prepared judges and well-prepared lawyers make for a better day, a good and true outcome, and respect from those we are there to serve.

Preparation is not a choice; it is a necessity. The judicial beatitudes are not like a buffet. We don't pick out our favorites; we are called to fully embrace all of these beatitudes. The people we serve need and deserve a judge who is well prepared.

Chapter 3

A Judge Should Be Diligent

Diligence by the judiciary is a necessity. A judge must be diligent in all he or she does. The lives of the people affected by your work deserve the highest level of diligence.

DOES DILIGENCE DEFINE YOUR JUDICIAL work ethic? Is your level of diligence one you would be comfortable with from a judge hearing crucial issues affecting your family or business? These questions are pointed, as they must be; the work you are charged with requires purposeful diligence in every aspect of your service to the public. The lives of your fellow man and the honor of the judiciary ride upon your level of diligence.

Diligent is defined as "characterized by steady, earnest, and energetic effort: painstaking." Would you say you are characterized as steady, earnest, energetic, and painstaking? Clearly those are characteristics we would want for the judge in our own case, right? To be a diligent judge is to be what any right-thinking person would want in a judge. Now, turn it around—would you want to be known as a judge who is not earnest, not energetic? Would you prefer your judicial epithet to read: Diligent or Idle?

A judge has the unique position of overseeing people in some of life's most trying moments. The vast majority of people who appear in the courts are there for a once-in-a-lifetime experience. They need and deserve judges who are diligent in their profession.

You may best remember the one or two "big cases" your career has brought before you. But your judicial epithet will not be decided by the "big cases"; your service will be defined by your diligence day in and day out. A judge serves the people best and elevates the judiciary by diligent daily service.

Diligence involves knowing the docket and seeing to the timely disposition of the cases coming before you. When the lawyers say, "Judge, we are both in agreement to continue this case if that is alright with you." Our first internal reaction is something like "Is it alright—are you kidding me? I would give anything to have a day off in the middle of this busy court term." What we actually say is something like this: "Well, if you have given this careful consideration and both of you think this is best, the court will not stand in your way." Diligence demands digging deeper; the lawyers may be in agreement, but what the clients need and deserve may be anything but another delay.

A judge's calling is one that both needs and deserves due diligence. We should want, in every way, to answer the call to serve on the bench with diligence. May we answer our calling, if this is our first day or our thirtieth year, with a high level of diligence by being careful, attentive, persistent, and earnest in our work. We owe ourselves the responsibility of diligence, and the people who come before us need and deserve nothing less.

Chapter 4

A Judge Should Be Wise

Judges need to be wise in thought, word, and deed. Judges are required to read and know the law, but wisdom goes beyond just knowing the law. The wisdom necessary for the art of judging is acquired over a lifetime of learning by studying but also by experiencing and observing life. There have been many who have gone before us whose writing and their very lives demonstrate wisdom. We do well to study them all. Wisdom is a foundational key to a judge's service. Judges must use their hearts, minds, and mouths judiciously and wisely.

WISDOM IS KNOWLEDGE GAINED FROM experiences in life; it is an acquired ability to see and understand things that many others cannot. Wisdom is having a knowledge of what is proper and reasonable, also known as "good sense." Wisdom and intelligence are not the same. Certainly a judge must be intelligent, but a judge who would serve the people well must also be wise.

Wisdom is an absolutely foundational quality for a judge. Judges regularly find themselves facing circumstances for which no course or classroom or colleague's advice can fully prepare. Judges face these uniquely challenging circumstances before a "live audience" with every word being recorded. A judge certainly needs to be intelligent, but even more so a judge must have and use wisdom. The wisdom a judge needs is acquired through many life experiences and a careful study of wise men and women who have lived throughout the ages.

The ultimate story of wisdom is the biblical account of King Solomon and the seemingly impossible case of two women claiming the same child as their own. Solomon had no idea which woman was the real mother, and there were no DNA tests available. Solomon's wisdom gave him a test more definitive than any modern science could offer. Solomon called for a sword to divide the child and allow both of the women to share equally. The first woman quickly agreed to the plan, but the other woman cried out in great anguish, "No!" The second woman's response clearly revealed to Solomon she was the real mother of the baby. Solomon was very wise in formulating a plan on how to discern the truth of these two women's competing claims to be the child's mother. Solomon did not learn the technique in a class; it was a wise decision born of his studies and his experience. The dilemma Solomon faced is one daily encountered by the judiciary. Judges face seemingly impossible situations daily! Wisdom is the key to finding one's way through the maze of judicial challenges.

While waiting to merge onto I-10 in Ocean Springs, Mississippi, I saw a personalized car tag with these letters: "icinsidu." This personalized tag intrigued me, and while I sat pondering the message, it dawned on me this must be a person working in the field of radiology. They "see inside you," so to speak. Oh how judges wish they had a machine that allowed us to "icinsidu." There is no such machine. The only thing that comes close is wisdom naturally and intentionally gained and applied at the bar of justice. A judge's attentiveness and application of wise principles are tools that equip him or her to better ascertain who is being truthful, to know what is going on inside the person, and to make correct decisions.

Wisdom is somewhat a gift, but more so it is an acquired trait. Wisdom is gained largely through living life with our eyes open, through personal observation and study of human behavior. Judges need to be people who have experienced real life, not people who live detached from the slings and arrows of real life and all its ups and downs. Every experience, good and bad, that comes our way helps to form our personality and give us a growing insight into people, their actions and motivations. Seeing life and all its challenges and learning from the process; reading the accounts of others and their responses to life—these are all paths to wisdom.

The hardest times in our lives present the greatest opportunity to grow in wisdom. Allow yourself to view your darkest hours and think on the lessons learned in those times. Living watchfully through the "dark night of your soul" is one of the greatest keys to acquiring real wisdom. Life's lessons, when properly viewed, help us to grow in wisdom, an acquired wisdom that is woven into the very fabric of our beings. This acquired knowledge can help us see and understand the difficult moments in the lives of others. Judges are first of all people who, if they are to serve wisely, will bring to bear their own life experiences. The judge's wisdom, properly viewed and applied, equips the judge to serve others more effectively.

Wisdom comes from intentionally choosing and studying the lives and writings of wise and experienced people. These people can certainly be those who we encounter in daily life; however, I find I am best served by studying the ancients, those whose wisdom is well known, tried, and proven. There are modern person-alities and writers who contribute greatly to the body of wisdom literature, and we must learn from them as well. Reading the works of men and women who have gained great wisdom from life's experiences is integral to the process of growing in wisdom in our own lives and service.

Wisdom is gained by listening. Judges enjoy speak-ing but gain much deeper and more productive insight with the ears than with the mouth. Attentive observa-tion and keen listening are most productive for gain-ing an accurate insight into what is really going on in court. When judges patiently and carefully listen, peo-ple, through what they say and what they don't say, allow us to "see inside." Judges gain greater insight by listening rather than by talking. I can vividly recall the times I felt compelled to speak, when listening would have better served the cause. Judges exercise and demonstrate wisdom and learn quite a bit by quiet-ly watching and listening. The old railroad crossbuck sign said it all: "Stop, Look, Listen." There is wisdom in those simple words.

There is a great lesson we can learn from this quote:

"Even fools are thought wise if they keep si-lent, and discerning if they hold their tongues"
(Proverbs 17:28).

I have found other judges to be a great source of wisdom and insight. Listening to them speak of their work is a reliable source of acquired wisdom. I confess a desire to tell my story, but when I am talking, I learn nothing; when I listen, the learning curve goes up significantly. We also gain wisdom and insight by listening to others in the judicial system. I have learned some great truths and helpful perspectives by carefully listening to court reporters, court administrators, clerks, deputy clerks, bailiffs, and other officers in the judicial system.

We can also learn quite a bit about ourselves by listening. If we open our minds to learn, as Moses did from Jethro, we will gain wisdom and insight into particular cases, the system itself, what kind of judges we are, and how to move toward the judges we really want and need to become.

When it comes to deciding cases, it is my opinion that this tool—the full gamut of wisdom—is one of the most important tools we have, if not *the* most important. A key to being a wise judge is listening to wisdom from above and having an honest recognition that there is much we don't know. More listening, more studying, more careful observation is a good road to making wise decisions.

Chapter 5

A Judge Should Be On Time

**Judges who respect everyone's time and
are themselves on time demonstrate
a servant's heart and respect for
all. Judges must be on time.**

"THEY CAN'T START WITHOUT YOU!" is a standing joke universally told to judges. The problem is many judges actually believe this is true. They begin to practice this principle of judging being all about the judge. Judges allow themselves to begin to believe the judicial system revolves around them.

This is not "our court," "our docket," or "our timetable." The right time to start court is not when "I get there"; this approach puts the judge in the center, and the system revolves around the judge. This approach is not judicial; it is a self-centered and prideful approach. This is not our system; we are here to serve and to serve properly, and we have to be on time!

The entire train of thought that proceeds along the path of "my court," "my docket," "my cases," and the like is inherently flawed. We have to totally eradicate such thought patterns from our way of viewing the judiciary. Judges are positioned, by election or appointment, to serve the people. Serving the people means we begin from this point of view: "What are the needs of those coming into the courts, and how can I help meet those needs?" The issue is not what we want, but what we are here to do in service to others. If the court session is scheduled to begin at nine, the judge needs to be present and ready well in advance of nine.

When we as judges are repeatedly late, it reflects a lack of respect and honor for the needs and rights of others. In other words, it is a complete failure of the very things we are here for. Life and time are precious. Nowhere is this more true than in the courts where people are anxiously awaiting their opportunity to be heard. With rare exception, the people sitting in the courtrooms have already had to wait too long for their story to be told. If judges flagrantly disregard the start time (whether in the morning or any other time during the court session), then we are choosing to ignore the rights and needs of others. When we are not respectful of the time, instead of healing we are causing further harm. This should not be; it cannot be—we must respect and honor the rights of those whom we are here to serve.

Judges owe a duty of timeliness to all who serve in the judicial system with us. The clerks, court reporters, bailiffs, and lawyers all need and deserve to have judges who are consistently on time. The lawyers depend on being able to take care of matters in a timely manner, allowing them to move on to other things. Judges who start on time and work to stay on time are showing respect to all the people we serve. Being on time is just basic good manners; it is an effort we owe to all.

Finally, being on time is good for the judges. When we demonstrate our attentiveness to our profession and all we serve, we feel better about our service. The judiciary that operates in a timely manner is helping to demonstrate the health and vitality of the entire judicial system. Judges who set an example by consistently being on time and thus showing respect to all are helping to rebuild and enhance the very system they serve.

Judges will be late. When we are late, here is what we should do: Apologize. "Ladies and gentlemen, I want to apologize to you for my tardiness this morning. It is my duty to respect all of you by being here on time. I was late this morning, and I regret any problems that my late arrival may have caused you. Please accept my apology." We owe this honest and respectful approach to everyone. Additionally, on the occasion when we are late and we admit and apologize, we actually make a positive out of the negative by our candor about our own human frailties. The judge who candidly admits and apologizes for being tardy is building both confidence and respect. The integrity of the bench is greatly enhanced when we are completely honest. A judge is "his honor" when he honors those who are being served. A simple way to honor others is by respecting their time by our own consistent timeliness.

Chapter 6

A Judge Should Be Humble

The noble art of judging is built upon the principle of humble service. The system does not exist to serve the judge; the most basic foundational principle of the judicial system is judges who are humbly serving all the people who come seeking justice.

HUMILITY IN SERVICE IS A principle upon which the art of the judiciary is founded. *Humility* is defined as "the quality of not thinking you are better than other people; having a modest view of one's own importance." My favorite definition of *humility* is this: "not thinking less of yourself, but thinking of yourself less." I would further define or describe humility for a judge as: Don't get caught up in the "Your Honor" business—it is not about you; it is about the position in which you serve and the people who come seeking justice.

There is a devastating and destructive judicial disease that has been called "robeitis." When a person who is placed in a position of trust to serve others as a judge contracts this destructive condition, it prevents any effective service by the infected person. The judge who suffers from "robeitis" sadly causes suffering to everyone else around them. In the well-known words of former Supreme Court Justice Potter Stewart, "robeitis" may be hard to define, but you know it immediately when you see it. The only cure for this disease is true humility. The opposite of humility is pride, and it is beyond dispute that *"pride goes before destruction" (Proverbs 16:18)*.

The Bible proclaims repeatedly that God hates pride, and pride is likewise highly offensive to people who have to put up with it. Here is an old but still important saying: "Judges may be elected or appointed, but they are never anointed." Get over yourself and settle down, get to work on the real business of judging—serving the people before you. This job is not our launching pad to greatness; if we are doing our job properly, it is our entryway into servanthood.

A judge has a duty to maintain order and decorum in the halls of justice, and particularly in his or her courtroom. The maintenance of proper respect for the system and its officers is important and cannot be ignored. However, the judge must not take himself or herself too seriously—we are not the system; we are servants of the system.

My judicial hero, Honorable R. B. Reeves (former Chancellor of the Fourth Chancery Court district), has said something like "When I get home, Gail hands me a broom and I sweep." He kept his place in life in perspective. He didn't take himself too seriously. He understood he was a public servant, and an exceptional one by my observation. He humbly and quite admirably served as judge for twelve years. Judge Reeves knew his robe was just a uniform he wore to serve others, not a badge of pride. He was elected, not anointed. We all might learn great lessons from his service and the service of many of you who have served and continue to serve with humility.

Chapter 7

A Judge Should Be Prompt

**Justice delayed is truly justice denied.
Judges must not put off until tomorrow what
can be done today. The business before
us is not ours to delay. Justice cries out
for timely delivery. Judges must seriously
endeavor to be prompt in their work!**

PICTURE THIS COURTROOM SCENE: It's late on Thursday afternoon, it has been a busy week, and a lawyer comes to the podium and says, "Your Honor, we are all tired, and we are not sure if we will be able to finish our case this week. With the court's permission we would like to just take tomorrow off and get with the court administrator and get a date to resume this matter sometime next month?" The judge is tired too and strongly inclined to go along with the lawyer's request. However, a careful glance at the parties sitting at counsel table reveals the look of anything but relief. There is no joy in the eyes or the hearts of the litigants. They are the ones we are all here to serve, but they are not the ones who want to continue the case. One of the most important lessons we can ever learn is simply this: Cases are never just cases; they are legal disputes that impact the lives of real people in very real and often hurtful ways.

Judges should promptly handle the matters before them. With rare exceptions, the cases that come before us are matters of high importance to the people affected by them. Delaying the final disposition of a case is sometimes desirable to one side of the dispute that welcomes a delay of what appears to be the inevitable. The one who wants and needs a final resolution is almost invariably hurt by further delay. Judges need to be aware and sensitive to these competing needs. While judges should respect the requests of the attorneys, judges must exercise wisdom and caution in the delay of justice. A judge has to know when and be willing to just say, "No!" Judges are charged with the responsibility of a prompt and timely adjudication of the matters before them.

"Under Advisement" is a hard place to leave litigants for any length of time. Judges often need to "take matters under advisement." The trial is over, but for various reasons the matter cannot be decided immediately. In taking the case under advisement, the judge is being careful, needs more time to research the issues, or, maybe he or she is pressed by other matters awaiting immediate adjudication. Any one of these may be a proper reason to temporarily delay a final decision. We call it "being careful," and often it is just that; we have heard the evidence and rather than rush into a decision at the end of a long day or in the middle of a day loaded with other cases, we simply say we will take the matter under advisement and issue a written opinion as soon as possible. When we take a matter under advisement, we are putting the people involved in a pressure-packed "waiting room," and they are left hanging while we go about our other duties.

The judge has good intentions when he or she takes a matter under advisement. Then tomorrow comes, and with it comes new "urgent matters"; the notes from the case under advisement get pushed to the side. Mail accumulates over several days and creates a mound over the notes that are now fading from the judge's memory. The accumulated mail eventually gets moved, but when the judge sees the notes, he or she thinks, "Oh, I will have to dig in here and remind myself of these facts, and I don't have time to do that right now. I will wait until the next time I have several days free, and I will reread all my notes and then get a decision out as soon as I can." Time marches on, and the "tyranny of the urgent" wrestles our attention away from the matter that is now on the back burner of our mind but is high on the hearts and minds of those waiting for the judge to make a decision that will greatly impact their lives. When a judge takes a matter under advisement, he or she is putting the lives of the people affected by that case on hold. Often, the people affected are not just the people before us but their families, children, business associates, and often many others who will be impacted by the judge's decision. Taking a matter under advisement may be necessary, but it must be done with caution and diligence and its resolution timely achieved.

Judges cannot allow matters to remain under advisement for lengthy periods of time. The lives and circumstances of the people they serve and others affected deserve and require a timely decision by the judge. Judges should, in almost all cases, get a decision out in no more than a week or two at very most. Certainly there are exceptions—and in those instances maybe a month is appropriate—but those cases should be rare, and the people need to be told promptly and accurately when to expect the judge's decision. With rare exception, it is simply unconscionable for a judge to keep a matter under advisement for lengthy periods of time.

When decisions are significantly delayed, no matter how good their notes are, some of the edge and perspective the judge had from actually hearing the case is lost. The perceptions gained from looking the witnesses in the eye and listening to the lawyers' best closing arguments fade significantly with time. The nature of our job and the significance of the matters at issue require that judges be prompt in our rulings. Justice delayed is always, at least to some extent, justice denied.

Chapter 8

A Judge Should Be Gentle

Judges can and must treat other people the way we want to be treated. We must treat all who come before us and all who work with us the very way we want and expect to be treated. Judges can and must treat other people with gentleness.

JUDGES HAVE FRONT-ROW SEATS AND a leading part in a theatre that often presents real-life human tragedy that has occurred and is still occurring in the lives of the participants. The matters before us are not cases on a docket; they are painful pages from the lives of the people appearing before us. Judges are thrust into the most difficult places in the lives of others who are going through some of the most sensitive and vulnerable moments they will ever experience. A judge's work significantly impacts the lives of others. This is something we should be vigilantly aware of, never losing sight of the critical nature of the toil of the judiciary. For these very reasons, the art of judging requires gentleness.

Gentleness is a quality that everyone admires. *Gentleness* is defined as "mildness of manner or disposition." Gentleness does not signify weakness or lack of authority; a calm and gentle judge reflects a clear understanding of the authority of the office and the seriousness of the matter at hand. Speaking and acting in a distraught or angry manner destroys our effectiveness and reflects negatively on the entire judicial system.

Maneuvering through life with gentleness to our fellow travelers is not something that just happens as we go. We have to be intentional in approaching others calmly and gently. Judges, more so than anyone else, need to get this; the people we encounter are almost always in crisis mode. A calm and steady judge is a gentle breeze in the lives of those who desperately need it. We need to be firmly committed to serving with an attitude of gentleness, thus carrying out this crucial judicial beatitude.

The art of judging often places a judge at the crossroads of life for the people appearing before the court. Judges can, and I suggest must, even in the most obstreperous of cases, conduct themselves with calm gentleness. There are people who appear before the court who are, by nature or circumstances of the case, disruptive and obnoxious. Judges must not, cannot respond in kind. Judges must be prepared in advance; before the "All rise, the Court of . . ." is ever pronounced, judges need to be aware we are about to encounter people about whom we must honestly say, "There but for the grace of God go I." When judges are prepared, they are able to carry out their duties with gentleness, even in the most trying circumstances.

When a judge fails to be gentle and maintain his or her equilibrium, the judge becomes a part of the problem. Judges should be the epitome of steady gentleness. If we fail in this role, we invite the whole proceeding to follow us down a bumpy and destructive road. This is a path a judge must not take nor allow the proceedings to go. A judge who is prepared, calm, deliberate, and gentle will keep the matter on track.

Judges encounter lawyers and litigants at their worst. Judges must not allow the hard and mean parts of their work to lead them into acting like the distraught litigant or lawyer with whom they are confronted. The people in front of us are having the worst of days, and we need to anticipate such conduct and be prepared to respond with gentleness. When judges, in the midst of all the controversy, remain calm, assured, and gentle, they deflate the situation and enable calmness to prevail.

Judges face facts and circumstances that are everything but gentle and calm. The duty of the judge does not change based on the fact pattern; the duty to go forward with a calm and gentle demeanor remains. The reality is this: It is in the most challenging cases that the judge's demeanor is most critical to both the flow and the outcome of the case and the lives of those involved. Judges have to prepare in advance to face and work through matters that literally squeeze the humanity out of the room. The only way for judges to carry out their jobs and maintain calm order in the process is to do so with strength in gentleness. The failsafe tool for judges in the midst of controversy is to maintain a calm, assured, purposeful, and gentle approach. A judge can and should exhibit gentleness even in the most challenging of matters.

Chapter 9

A Judge Should Be Kind

Kindness is appropriate in every facet of life; the art of judging is no exception. Judges can and must be kind in even the most difficult of circumstances. Judges can and must be kind to all the people all the time.

KINDNESS IS ONE OF THE greatest gifts we can give to people. Kindness is the quality of being considerate. How could we possibly argue with a duty to be kind? Who would want to be intentionally inconsiderate? Antonyms for *kindness* include cold-heartedness, mercilessness, and inhumanness; judges should not desire such a description of their life's work.

A judge's opportunities to demonstrate kindness are plentiful. In fact, I propose we have more opportunities to show kindness than almost any other profession. It is indisputable that kindness flowing from a judge will get high notice and deep appreciation. Judges can and should do the job before them fully in accordance with the legal and factual mandates of the case, yet with kindness to all. It grieves me to think back over the missed opportunities I had to bring kindness to bear where it was so much needed. I allowed the moment to pull me in and thus reacted in accordance with the prevailing mood. This should not be; this must not be. Judges have the responsibility to set the tone and set it high—set it with kindness.

Judges have opportunities from the parking lot to the bench to show kindness to many people—from the elderly lady heading in to pay her taxes to the down-and-out middle-aged man coming out the side door who just learned he owes a fine beyond his financial reach to court staff, reporters, bailiffs, and others. Judges have to commit themselves to acting with kindness to all we encounter. A judge who carries out all his or her duties with kindness to all will absolutely transform the way the litigants, the people, and the world around us see the entire judicial system. The judicial system is awaiting its transformation by judges living out these beatitudes, none more important than basic human kindness.

The judiciary is the third branch of government in America. We can, we should, and we must set the tone for all three branches of government. The judicial branch intersects with the lives of everyday people far more than the executive or legislative branches of government. Judges set the tone for their own judicial offices and their part of the judicial system. Judges, we have the chance to change the very direction of our nation and our world. The plan is not judicial activism; the plan is simple: Treat people the way they deserve to be treated. Treat the people who come into the courts with kindness.

A judge should be, no must be kind!

Chapter 10

A Judge Should Be Patient

Patience is a core principle for judging. Judges have to work patiently at their profession. When judges lose patience, their effort ceases to be an art; it ceases to be justice. The present moment is the most important moment in life—no one and nothing is more important than the present and the people who are before you. Judges must be patient to all in all they do.

W<small>E LIVE IN A WORLD</small> that is moving at the speed of . . . (I am not savvy enough to even describe the speed—it's a fast, fast world!) We want everything, and we want it now. The computer age has trained us to have zero patience and zero tolerance for anyone who isn't trying to get what they want at the speed of life. We live in a very impatient world.

Judges cannot and must not let the pace of the world control in the judiciary. Judges must patiently approach and engage with all who come in—the people whose business is before us; the witnesses, usually there against their wishes; the attorneys; and other people who are just there as observers. When we demonstrate patience and tolerance with the human side of all people, we are being truly judicial and wise in our conduct. Patience is not necessarily natural for all judges; however, patience is a must-have virtue for every judge. Many judges are not patient by nature, but it is the judge's duty to seek to develop patience in his or her service.

The quality of being patient is defined as "showing calm self-control, demonstrating forbearance under strain, not hasty." Patience as encountered in the laboratory of life is facing difficulties without losing your cool, your temper, or your wits. I have failed to exhibit patience on more occasions than I can recall. This is not a mistake I care to repeat. Judges are all called to be patient—we certainly are not called to lose our temper, to complain, or even to be irritated. A judge can and should control his or her courtroom without even a hint of impatience. In fact, if we really think of it, the very best way to maintain control and to efficiently move the business of the courts along is to do so with great patience. The very fact that patience has not been our greatest virtue should compel us to seek to be patient to all who come before us in the courts. Patience is a virtue that rewards all involved, including the judicial system itself.

I have heard judges say, "I am just not a patient person. I can't help it; I was just not born with patience." Respectfully, it is not a question of what the judge is born with; it is a matter of choosing how to respond to life as it occurs in our presence. The issue here is not our personality but our responsibility. We are responsible for maintaining peace and calm in the courts. There is no single principle more effective for bringing and keeping calm than patience.

Chapter 11

A Judge Should Be Honest

Judges have to be honest! Honesty should permeate every aspect of the art of judging. Judges must vigilantly guard against anything that gives even an appearance of undermining complete honesty in the judiciary.

IS THIS BEATITUDE SO OBVIOUS as to not require inclusion here? No! We must constantly and vigilantly guard the virtue of honesty in the judiciary. Judges must be unwaveringly scrupulous in all conduct, actions, and appearances. There are well-known and much publicized failures in the judiciary; this is because judges are human. The recognition that we are all human—that we all have our own frailties and such failures could be any one of us—is the real and compelling reason we must have an unwavering commitment to avoid even an appearance of impropriety.

We need to be honest in small and self-effacing ways: "We are starting late today because I just didn't get here on time," or "This case is being continued because I had to change my schedule for personal reasons," or "My decision was delayed because I didn't begin work on this as soon as I wanted and needed to," and the most needed and hardest, "I just plain got that wrong, and now I need to amend and change my earlier ruling to correct my error."

Judges, as is true of people in general, can always find ways to point the blame elsewhere. If we are honest in these small things, it signals to the public and those we regularly work with, "You can count on our judge; he or she is going to shoot straight all the time." This is monumental; it helps the entire system function properly. When people know they can count on their judge to be honest in all things, big and small, it makes the whole system healthier and allows it to operate at its very best.

We need and request complete candor from counsel and people appearing before us (you know that "whole truth and nothing but the truth, so help you God" thing), and we as judges have to give back that same level of candor. These may seem like small matters, but the truth is, if we lose credibility on these small points, it hurts our credibility in many ways, big and small. What's more, it has been my experience that when I just acknowledge my shortcomings, my failures, my oversights, it is appreciated, and the system, instead of getting a "black eye," gains esteem because of the candor of the judge.

When circumstances arise that create confusion and misunderstanding in the courtroom, there are several options but only one right answer. We need to address problems and misunderstandings head-on and in the open. We don't need to make excuses or attempt to avoid the troubling issues. If we as judges have made mistakes that created or contributed to the problem, acknowledge it, address it, resolve it, and move on. If one or more of the lawyers have created a problem, it is not our job or goal to skewer lawyers but to try to work through the challenge while maintaining our credibility and requiring the same of the lawyers.

Transparency by judges is, almost without exception, the right call. No matter the communication, no matter the issue, we owe complete fidelity to ourselves, the bench and bar, and the public we exist to serve. There have been so many "black eyes" to the judicial system; let's make sure we don't lay the groundwork for a "shiner" of any size. As serious-minded and dedicated judges, let's be scrupulously honest in all things. There will be times when we realize we have acted in a way that may reflect negatively on our service and the system we serve. When this happens, there is only one way to resolve the problem: acknowledge our mistake, address it, and move forward with honor. A judge must be unwaveringly honest in all matters, big and small.

Chapter 12

A Judge Should Be Fair

Fairness is the most foundational of all judicial principles. A judge must be fair to all, at all times and in all things. Judges must carefully listen, thoughtfully consider, and then fairly decide every matter.

BEING FAIR IS NOT LAST on this list by accident. To say a judge is fair is to give him or her the highest compliment a judge can receive. This is what all people ultimately want. If a judge is fair, he or she can overcome a deficit in some other areas; fairness is over all other judicial beatitudes. Yet in truth, fairness is simply the foundation upon which all the other judicial beatitudes rest. Without fairness, the others are essentially meaningless.

The people coming into the courts, the lawyers who will appear before you, all who come in contact with the court in which you serve will be at ease if they know the judge is fair. We need to—in fact, we must— embrace all of the beatitudes, but I think this one is the catchall of proper judicial attitudes. In the larger sense, it encompasses all of the beatitudes.

Fairness as a principle is characterized by these words: "just," "equitable," "upright," "honorable," "IMPARTIAL," "unbiased," and "evenhanded"! If we turn fairness inside out, what do we have? Unjust, biased, and dishonest! No right-thinking person ever wants to be characterized as unjust, biased, or dishonest! We want to work with great diligence and extreme care in conveying fairness in all we do and with all whom we come in contact.

Fair doesn't just apply to the ultimate decision; it is a term that needs to accompany our work from the time a case is filed until it is finally concluded. Fairness needs to describe all that we do, from our getting up to our lying down. The little things are not little; they are big, and we need to be fair in all. From calling our docket to addressing preliminary motions to dealing with matters that are very bothersome to all of us, in all of these our actions, our words, our attitudes need to demonstrate absolute fairness to all. We need to monitor our communications and even our body language, our every action to guard against any sense of favoritism or any conduct that transmits any message other than absolute fairness.

Justly or unjustly, sometimes we are not viewed as being absolutely fair in all we do. We must move beyond yesterday and make sure that on this day we endeavor in every means possible to serve with unblemished fairness in all we do. We don't need to coddle the one who may have branded us as unfair to win them back; we need to conduct ourselves this day with an absolute sense of fairness to all. Today is not the entire book of our judicial lives; it is one page out of the book. We need to endeavor to have today's page read, "Fair in every way!"

He or she is "a fair judge" is a light in which we all want to be cast. It is not others who cast the light on our work; it is cast by how we live our judicial lives. It is cast by years of conducting ourselves, day in and day out, in a certain manner both in and out of the courts. Neither the writer nor the readers of this work have always gotten this right. Today is the day in which we live and the day for us to live with complete fairness in all we do. We have to make fairness a top priority in all things at all times.

Conclusion

TO BE A JUDGE IS to answer the call to serve others. Judging is a calling and requires the heart of a servant who endeavors to live out all of these judicial beatitudes. No single one of the beatitudes is a standalone principle; a close inspection reveals every principle builds upon and is undergirded by the others.

The judicial beatitudes paint a portrait of the judge we should all seek to be—to become judges characterized by these beatitudes. This is not for the sake of the judge but for the sake of those whom he and she serve. I can say with complete candor, this is not a portrait of me, nor is it a portrait of any one judge I know. It is, in fact, a good portrait of the judge we should all aspire to be. If these beatitudes do not reflect our goals as judges, we might well reevaluate the principles we are using.

Judicial life is a journey. The goal of this writing is judicial excellence. Judicial excellence is a long process encompassing all of these beatitudes and more. The judiciary is the third branch of American government. Judges serve as the gatekeepers between citizens and those who would deprive them of their constitutional and other lawful rights. Judges are called to serve; it is here respectfully suggested these beatitudes represent good touchstones for us to tread upon as we journey through our judicial lives.

May the words of our mouths and the meditations of our hearts line up with the judicial beatitudes expounded here!

About the Author

HOLLIS MCGEHEE IS A RETIRED Mississippi Judge having served for many years as a Chancellor and Senior Status Judge. As Senior Status Judge Hollis served as a Youth Court Judge, Chancellor, Circuit Court Judge and Court of Appeals Judge. Earlier in his career he also served as a City Court Judge, Family Master and Youth Court Referee. Hollis is the father of three children, Caj McGehee, Simmons Copeland, and Abbay McGehee and five grandchildren. He currently makes his home on Black Creek in Brooklyn, Mississippi. He is the author of two prior works, *Follow Him in Thought* and *Word and Follow Him in All Things.* Judge McGehee is a native of Franklin County, Mississippi where he lived most of his life.